JAZZ PLAY ALONG

Book and CD for B♭, E♭ and C Instruments

RODGERS & HART FAVORITES

10 RODGERS & HART FAVORITES

Arranged and Produced by Mark Taylor

WILLIAMSON MUSIC is a registered trademark of the Family Trust u/w RichardRodgers, the Family Trust u/w Dorothy F. Rodgers and the Estate of Oscar Hammerstein II

Performance Disclaimer:
These arrangements and recordings are intended for private home use only. They may not be used in connection with any performance that includes the use of costumes, choreography or other elements that evoke the story or characters of a legitimate stage musical work.

ISBN 0-634-05357-4

WILLIAMSON MUSIC®

A RODGERS AND HAMMERSTEIN COMPANY

www.williamsonmusic.com

EXCLUSIVELY DISTRIBUTED BY

HAL•LEONARD® CORPORATION

7777 W. BLUEMOUND RD. P.O. BOX 13819 MILWAUKEE, WI 53213

Visit Hal Leonard Online at
www.halleonard.com

Rodgers & Hart Favorites

Arranged and Produced by
Mark Taylor

Featured Players:

Graham Breedlove-Trumpet
John Desalme-Alto Sax & Tenor Sax
Tony Nalker-Piano
Jim Roberts-Bass
Steve Fidyk-Drums

HOW TO USE THE CD:

Each song has <u>two</u> tracks:

1) Split Track/Melody

Woodwind, Brass, Keyboard, and Mallet Players can use this track as a learning tool for melody style and inflection.

Bass Players can learn and perform with this track – remove the recorded bass track by turning down the volume on the LEFT channel.

Keyboard and **Guitar Players** can learn and perform with this track – remove the recorded piano part by turning down the volume on the RIGHT channel.

2) Full Stereo Track

Soloists or **groups** can learn and perform with this accompaniment track with the RHYTHM SECTION only.

BEWITCHED

FROM PAL JOEY

WORDS BY LORENZ HART
MUSIC BY RICHARD RODGERS

CD
1: SPLIT TRACK/MELODY
2: FULL STEREO TRACK

C VERSION

THE BLUE ROOM
FROM THE GIRL FRIEND

WORDS BY LORENZ HART
MUSIC BY RICHARD RODGERS

CD
3: SPLIT TRACK/MELODY
4: FULL STEREO TRACK

C VERSION

I COULD WRITE A BOOK

FROM PAL JOEY

WORDS BY LORENZ HART
MUSIC BY RICHARD RODGERS

C VERSION

CD
9 : SPLIT TRACK/MELODY
10 : FULL STEREO TRACK

HAVE YOU MET MISS JONES?

FROM I'D RATHER BE RIGHT

WORDS BY LORENZ HART
MUSIC BY RICHARD RODGERS

C VERSION

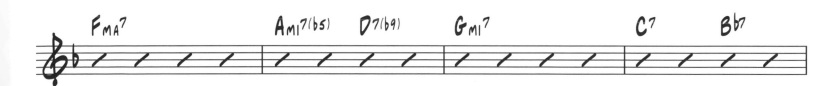

THE LADY IS A TRAMP
FROM BABES IN ARMS

WORDS BY LORENZ HART
MUSIC BY RICHARD RODGERS

C VERSION

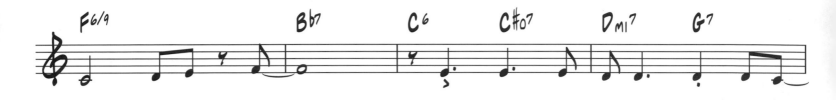

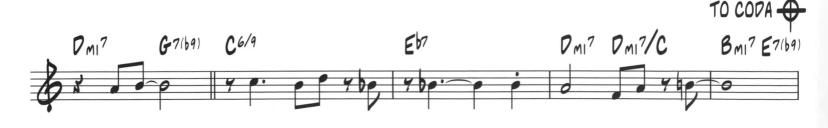

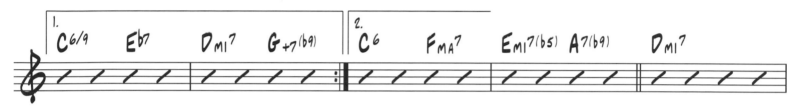

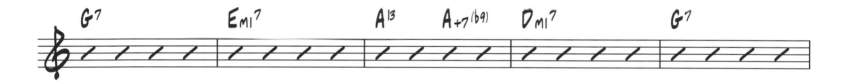

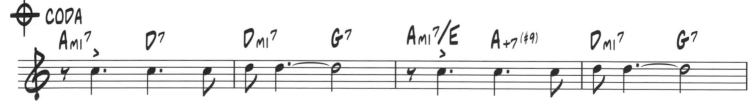

12

LITTLE GIRL BLUE
FROM JUMBO

WORDS BY LORENZ HART
MUSIC BY RICHARD RODGERS

C VERSION

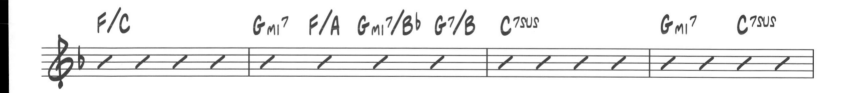

TO CODA

B mi7   Bb 13(#11)   A mi7   Ab 13(#11)   G 9sus   A mi7   D mi7   F ma7/G   G 13(b9)

(G 13(b9))

SOLOS
C ma7   F ma7   E mi7   A mi7   D mi7   G 7   C ma7   Bb 7

A mi   A mi(ma7)/G#   A mi7/G   Eb 9(#11)   D mi7   G 7   C ma7   G mi7   C 7(b9)

1.
F ma7   Bb 7   C ma7   G mi7 C 7(b9)   F ma7   Bb 7   C ma7   G mi7

F# mi7   B 7(b9)   E mi7   Bb 7   A mi7   D 7(b9)   G 7

2.
F ma7   Eb 9(#11)   D mi7   D mi7/C   B mi11   Bb 13(#11)   A mi9   Ab 13(#11)

D.S. AL CODA

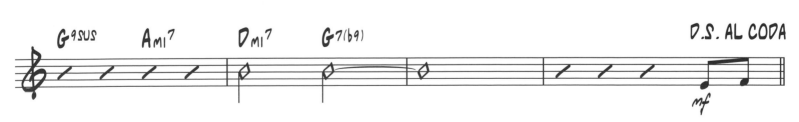

G 9sus   A mi7   D mi7   G 7(b9)

mf

CODA
3X'S   G 7(b9)

C ma7

CD
◆17◆ : SPLIT TRACK/MELODY
◆18◆ : FULL STEREO TRACK

THERE'S A SMALL HOTEL
FROM ON YOUR TOES

WORDS BY LORENZ HART
MUSIC BY RICHARD RODGERS

C VERSION

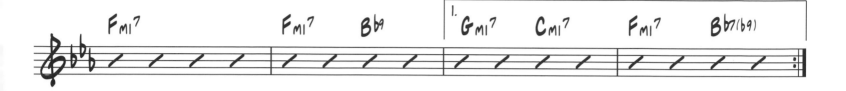

*SOLOS

| Eb MA7 | | Eb MA7 Ab7 | G MI7 Gbo7 |

| F MI7 | F MI7 Bb9 | 1. G MI7 C MI7 | F MI7 Bb7(b9) |

| 2. Eb7 | Bb MI7 A7 | Ab MA7 F MI7 | Bb MI7 Eb7 |

| Ab MA7 | G MI7 C7 | F MI7 | G MI7 C7 | Gb9 F MI7 |

| Cb9 Bb9 | Eb MA7 | Eb MA7 Ab7 | G MI7 Gbo7 |

D.S. AL CODA

| F MI7 | F MI7 Bb7 | Eb MA7 | F MI7 Bb7(b9) |

(BACK TO * FOR MORE SOLOS)

⊕ CODA

| F MI7 | Bb7SUS Bb7(b9) | Gb MA7 | Ab MI7 Db7 |

| Bb7SUS | | Bb7SUS | Eb MA9 |

You Are Too Beautiful

FROM HALLELUJAH, I'M A BUM

WORDS BY LORENZ HART
MUSIC BY RICHARD RODGERS

D♭ₘₐ⁷   Cₘₐ⁹
(-)

RIT.

BEWITCHED
FROM PAL JOEY

WORDS BY LORENZ HART
MUSIC BY RICHARD RODGERS

THE BLUE ROOM
FROM THE GIRL FRIEND

WORDS BY LORENZ HART
MUSIC BY RICHARD RODGERS

B♭ VERSION

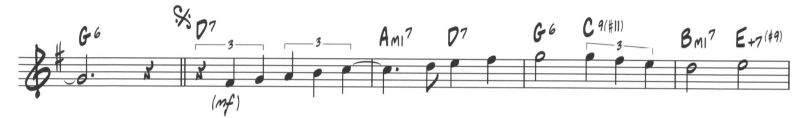

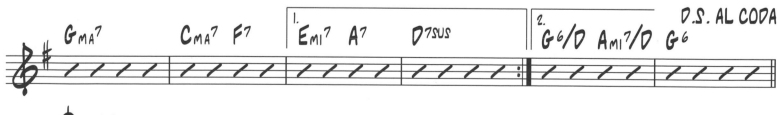

DANCING ON THE CEILING
FROM SIMPLE SIMON

WORDS BY LORENZ HART
MUSIC BY RICHARD RODGERS

I COULD WRITE A BOOK

FROM PAL JOEY

WORDS BY LORENZ HART
MUSIC BY RICHARD RODGERS

CD
7: SPLIT TRACK/MELODY
8: FULL STEREO TRACK

Bb VERSION

HAVE YOU MET MISS JONES?
FROM I'D RATHER BE RIGHT

WORDS BY LORENZ HART
MUSIC BY RICHARD RODGERS

25

CD
- 11 : SPLIT TRACK/MELODY
- 12 : FULL STEREO TRACK

THE LADY IS A TRAMP
FROM BABES IN ARMS

WORDS BY LORENZ HART
MUSIC BY RICHARD RODGERS

Bb VERSION

TO CODA ⊕

CD

13 : SPLIT TRACK/MELODY
14 : FULL STEREO TRACK

LITTLE GIRL BLUE
FROM JUMBO

WORDS BY LORENZ HART
MUSIC BY RICHARD RODGERS

B♭ VERSION

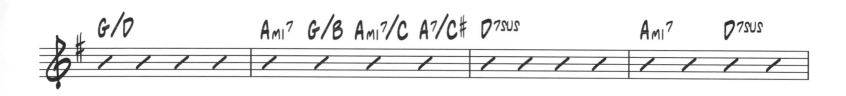

CD

15 : SPLIT TRACK/MELODY
16 : FULL STEREO TRACK

MY ROMANCE
FROM JUMBO

WORDS BY LORENZ HART
MUSIC BY RICHARD RODGERS

B♭ VERSION

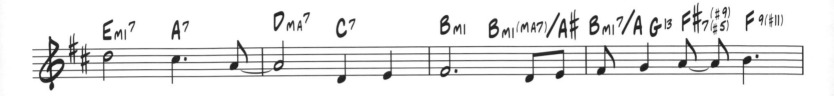

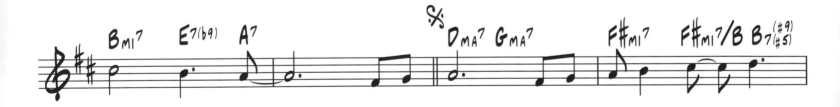

TO CODA
C♯mi7 C13(♯11) Bmi7 Bb13(♯11) A9sus Bmi7 Emi7 Gma7/A A13(b9)
(A13(b9))
SOLOS
Dma7 Gma7 F♯mi7 Bmi7 Emi7 A7 Dma7 C7
Bmi Bmi(ma7)/A♯ Bmi7/A F9(♯11) Emi7 A7 Dma7 Ami7 D7(b9)
1.
Gma7 C7 Dma7 Ami7 D7(b9) Gma7 C7 Dma7 Ami7
G♯mi7 C♯7(b9) F♯mi7 C7 Bmi7 E7(b9) A7
2.
Gma7 F9(♯11) Emi7 Emi7/D C♯mi11 C13(♯11) Bmi9 Bb13(♯11)
A9sus Bmi7 Emi7 A7(b9)
D.S. AL CODA
mf
CODA
3X'S A7(b9)
Dma7

THERE'S A SMALL HOTEL
FROM ON YOUR TOES

WORDS BY LORENZ HART
MUSIC BY RICHARD RODGERS

CD
17: SPLIT TRACK/MELODY
18: FULL STEREO TRACK

Bb VERSION

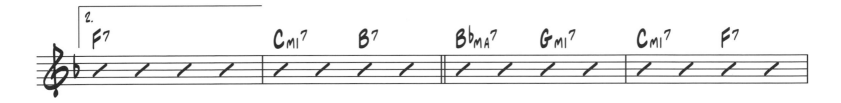

D.S. AL CODA

(BACK TO ✱ FOR MORE SOLOS)

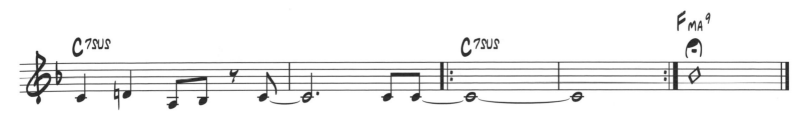

You Are Too Beautiful

FROM HALLELUJAH, I'M A BUM

WORDS BY LORENZ HART
MUSIC BY RICHARD RODGERS

CD
19 : SPLIT TRACK/MELODY
20 : FULL STEREO TRACK

Bb VERSION

BEWITCHED
FROM PAL JOEY

WORDS BY LORENZ HART
MUSIC BY RICHARD RODGERS

THE BLUE ROOM

FROM THE GIRL FRIEND

WORDS BY LORENZ HART
MUSIC BY RICHARD RODGERS

Eb VERSION

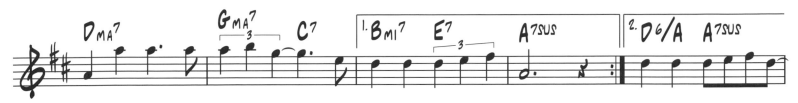

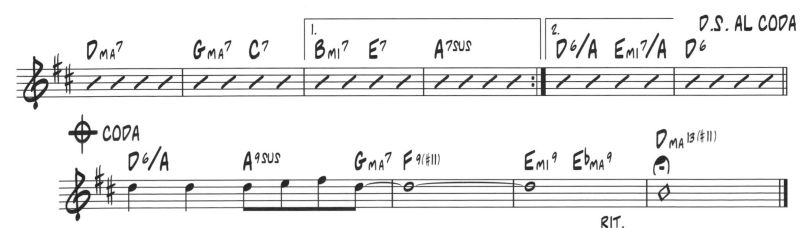

DANCING ON THE CEILING

FROM SIMPLE SIMON

WORDS BY LORENZ HART
MUSIC BY RICHARD RODGERS

I COULD WRITE A BOOK

FROM PAL JOEY

WORDS BY LORENZ HART
MUSIC BY RICHARD RODGERS

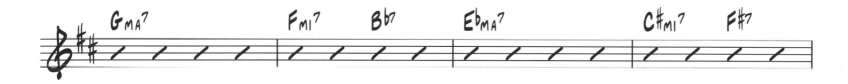

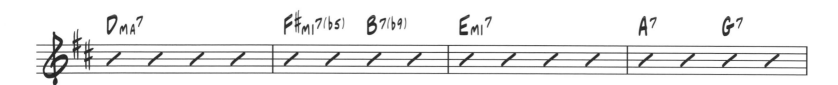

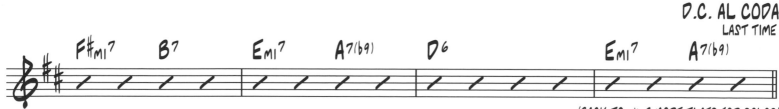

(BACK TO ✱ 2 MORE TIMES FOR SOLOS)

CD
11: SPLIT TRACK/MELODY
12: FULL STEREO TRACK

THE LADY IS A TRAMP
FROM BABES IN ARMS

WORDS BY LORENZ HART
MUSIC BY RICHARD RODGERS

E♭ VERSION

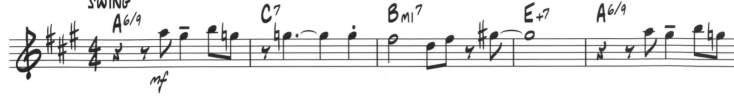

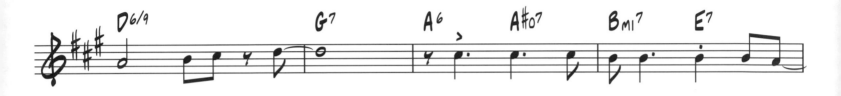

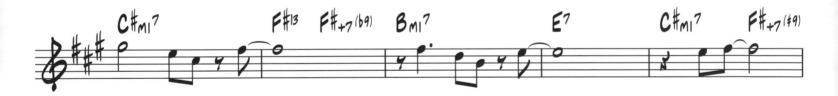

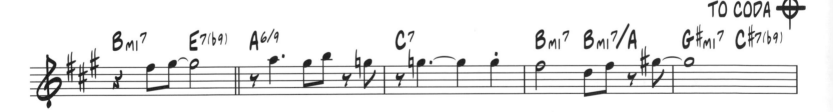

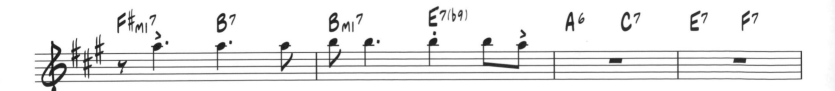

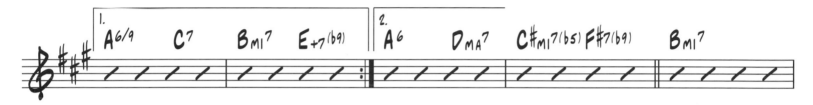

LITTLE GIRL BLUE
FROM JUMBO

WORDS BY LORENZ HART
MUSIC BY RICHARD RODGERS

E♭ VERSION

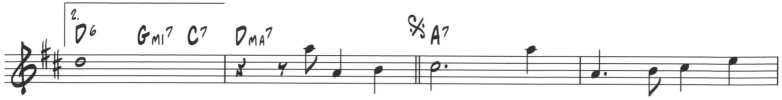

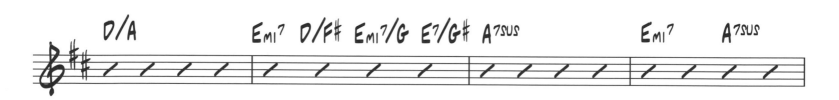

MY ROMANCE
FROM JUMBO

WORDS BY LORENZ HART
MUSIC BY RICHARD RODGERS

TO CODA ⊕

Line 1: G#mi7 — G13(#11) — F#mi7 — F13(#11) — E9sus — F#mi7 — Bmi7 — Dma7/E — E13(b9)

Line 2: (E13(b9)) — SOLOS — Ama7 — Dma7 — C#mi7 — F#mi7 — Bmi7 — E7 — Ama7 — G7

Line 3: F#mi — F#mi(ma7)/F — F#mi7/E — C9(#11) — Bmi7 — E7 — Ama7 — Emi7 — A7(b9)

Line 4 [1.]: Dma7 — G7 — Ama7 — Emi7 — A7(b9) — Dma7 — G7 — Ama7 — Emi7

Line 5: D#mi7 — G#7(b9) — C#mi7 — G7 — F#mi7 — B7(b9) — E7

Line 6 [2.]: Dma7 — C9(#11) — Bmi7 — Bmi7/A — G#mi11 — G13(#11) — F#mi9 — F13(#11)

Line 7: E9sus — F#mi7 — Bmi7 — E7(b9) — D.S. AL CODA — *mf*

⊕ CODA
3X'S E7(b9) — Ama7 (-)

THERE'S A SMALL HOTEL

FROM ON YOUR TOES

WORDS BY LORENZ HART
MUSIC BY RICHARD RODGERS

CD
17 : SPLIT TRACK/MELODY
18 : FULL STEREO TRACK

C VERSION

You Are Too Beautiful

FROM HALLELUJAH, I'M A BUM

WORDS BY LORENZ HART
MUSIC BY RICHARD RODGERS

Eb VERSION

BEWITCHED
FROM PAL JOEY

WORDS BY LORENZ HART
MUSIC BY RICHARD RODGERS

Dancing on the Ceiling
FROM SIMPLE SIMON

WORDS BY LORENZ HART
MUSIC BY RICHARD RODGERS

I COULD WRITE A BOOK
FROM PAL JOEY

WORDS BY LORENZ HART
MUSIC BY RICHARD RODGERS

HAVE YOU MET MISS JONES?

FROM I'D RATHER BE RIGHT

CD
◆ 9 : SPLIT TRACK/MELODY
◇ 10 : FULL STEREO TRACK

WORDS BY LORENZ HART
MUSIC BY RICHARD RODGERS

𝄢: C VERSION

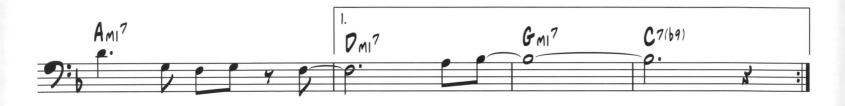

57

SOLO BREAK ✳ SOLOS
F MA7 A MI7(b5) D7(b9)

G MI7 C7 A MI7 D MI7

1. G MI7 C7(b9) 2. C MI7 F7

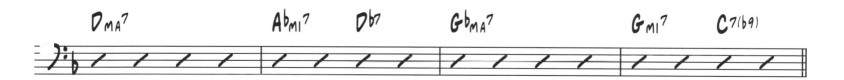

Bb MA7 Ab MI7 Db7 Gb MA7 E MI7 A7

D MA7 Ab MI7 Db7 Gb MA7 G MI7 C7(b9)

F MA7 A MI7(b5) D7(b9) G MI7 C7 Bb7

D.C. AL CODA
LAST TIME

A MI7 D7 G MI7 C7(b9) F6 G MI7 C7(b9)

(BACK TO ✳ 2 MORE TIMES FOR SOLOS)

⊕ CODA F MA9

CD
11 : SPLIT TRACK/MELODY
12 : FULL STEREO TRACK

THE LADY IS A TRAMP
FROM BABES IN ARMS

WORDS BY LORENZ HART
MUSIC BY RICHARD RODGERS

𝄢: C VERSION

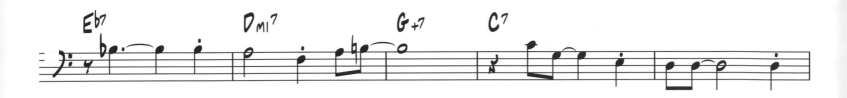

LITTLE GIRL BLUE

FROM JUMBO

WORDS BY LORENZ HART
MUSIC BY RICHARD RODGERS

9: C VERSION

MY ROMANCE

FROM JUMBO

WORDS BY LORENZ HART
MUSIC BY RICHARD RODGERS

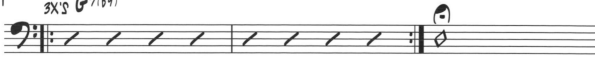

THERE'S A SMALL HOTEL

FROM ON YOUR TOES

WORDS BY LORENZ HART
MUSIC BY RICHARD RODGERS

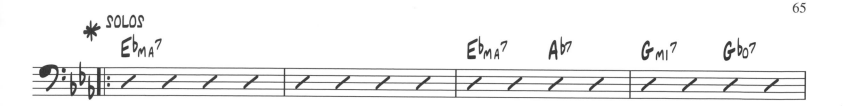

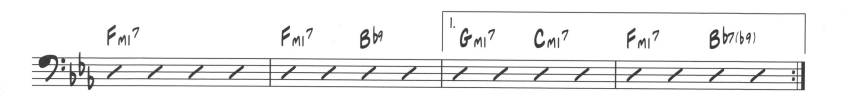

(BACK TO ✳ FOR MORE SOLOS)

YOU ARE TOO BEAUTIFUL

FROM HALLELUJAH, I'M A BUM

WORDS BY LORENZ HART
MUSIC BY RICHARD RODGERS

Lyrics

BEWITCHED

He's a fool and don't I know it,
But a fool can have his charms.
I'm in love and don't I show it
Like a babe in arms.
Love's the same old sad sensation,
Lately I've not slept a wink
Since this half-pint imitation
Put me on the blink.

I'm wild again, beguiled again,
A simpering, whimpering child again,
Bewitched,
Bothered and bewildered am I.
Couldn't sleep and wouldn't sleep
When love came and told me
I shouldn't sleep,
Bewitched,
Bothered and bewildered am I.
Lost my heart, but what of it?
He is cold, I agree.
He's a laugh, but I love it
Although the laugh's on me.
I'll sing to him, each spring to him,
And long for the day
When I cling to him,
Bewitched,
Bothered and bewildered am I.

THE BLUE ROOM

All my future plans,
Dear, will not suit your plans.
Read the little blueprints.
Here's your mother's room.
Here's your brother's room.
On the wall are two prints.
Here's the kiddie's room,
Here's the biddy's room,
Here's a pantry lined with shelves, dear.
Here I've planned for us
Something grand for us,
Where we two can be ourselves, dear.

We'll have a blue room,
A new room, for two room,
Where every day's a holiday,
Because you're married to me.
Not like a ballroom,
A small room, a hall room,
Where I can smoke my pipe away
With your wee head upon my knee.
We will thrive on,
Keep alive on,
Just nothing but kisses,
With Mister and Missus
On little blue chairs.

You sew your trousseau,
And Robinson Crusoe
Is not so far from worldly cares
As our blue room far away upstairs.

From all visitors
And inquisitors
We'll keep our apartment.
I won't change your plans-
You arrange your plans
Just the way your heart meant.
Here we'll be ourselves
And we'll see ourselves
Doing all the things we're scheming.
Here's a certain place,
Cretonne curtain place,
Where no one can see us dreaming.

DANCING ON THE CEILING

The world is lyrical
Because a miracle
Has brought my lover to me!
Though he's some other place,
His face I see.
At night I creep in bed,
And never sleep in bed,
But look above in the air.
And to my greatest joy,
My boy is there!
It is my prince who walks
Into my dreams and talks.

He dances overhead
On the ceiling, near my bed,
In my sight, through the night.

I try to hide in vain,
Underneath my counterpane,
There's my love, up above!

I whisper, "Go away, my lover,
It's not fair,"
But I'm so grateful to discover
He's still there.
I love my ceiling more
Since it is a dancing floor,
Just for my love.

HAVE YOU MET MISS JONES?

It happened, I felt it happen.
I was awake, I wasn't blind.
I didn't think, I felt it happen.
Now I believe in matter over mind.
And you see we mustn't wait.
The nearest moment
That we marry is too late!

"Have you met Miss Jones?"
Someone said as we shook hands.
She was just Miss Jones to me.
Then I said, "Miss Jones,
You're a girl who understands
I'm a man who must be free."
And all at once I lost my breath.
And all at once was scared to death.
And all at once
I owned the earth and sky!
Now I've met Miss Jones
And we'll keep on meeting till we die,
Miss Jones and I.

I COULD WRITE A BOOK

A B C D E F G
I never learned to spell,
At least not well.
1 2 3 4 5 6 7
I never learned to count
A great amount.
But my busy mind is burning
To use what learning I've got.
I won't waste any time,
I'll strike while the iron is hot.

If they asked me, I could write a book
About the way you walk
And whisper and look.
I could write a preface on how we met
So the world would never forget.

And the simple secret of the plot
Is just to tell them that I love you a lot.
Then the world discovers
As my book ends
How to make two lovers of friends.

Used to hate to go to school.
I never cracked a book;
I played the hook.
Never answered any mail;
To write I used to think
Was wasting ink.
It was never my endeavor
To be too clever and smart.
Now I suddenly feel
A longing to write in my heart.

THE LADY IS A TRAMP

I've wined and dined on Mulligan stew
And never wished for turkey
As I hitched and hiked and grifted too,
From Maine to Albuquerque.
Alas, I missed the Beaux Arts Ball,
And what is twice as sad,
I was never at a party
Where they honored No'l Ca'ad.
But social circles spin too fast for me.
My hobohemia is the place for me

I get too hungry for dinner at eight.
I like the theatre, but never come late.
I never bother with people I hate.
That's why the lady is a tramp.
I don't like crap games
With barons and earls.
Won't go to Harlem
In ermine and pearls.
Won't dish the dirt
With the rest of the girls.
That's why the lady is a tramp.
I like the free, fresh wind in my hair,
Life without care.
I'm broke-it's oke.
Hate California-it's cold and damp.
That's why the lady is a tramp.

I go to Coney-the beach is divine.
I go to ball games-the bleachers are fine.
I follow Winchell and read every line.
That's why the lady is a tramp.
I like a prizefight that isn't a fake.
I love the rowing on Central Park Lake.
I go to operas and stay wide awake.
That's why the lady is a tramp.
I like the green grass under my shoes.
What can I lose?
I'm flat! That's that!
I'm all alone when I lower my lamp.
That's why the lady is a tramp.

Don't know the reason
For cocktails at five.
I don't like flying-I'm glad I'm alive.
I crave affection, but not when I drive.
That's why the lady is a tramp.
Folks go to London
And leave me behind.
I missed the crowning,
Queen Mary won't mind.
I don't play Scarlett
In Gone with the Wind.

That's why the lady is a tramp.
I like to hang my hat where I please.
Sail with the breeze.
No dough-heigh-ho!
I love La Guardia
And think he's a champ.
That's why the lady is a tramp.

Girls get massages,
They cry and they moan.
Tell Lizzie Arden to leave me alone.
I'm not too hot,
But my shape is my own.
That's why the lady is a tramp!
The food at Sardi's is perfect, no doubt.
I wouldn't know what the Ritz is about.
I drop a nickel and coffee comes out.
That's why the lady is a tramp!
I like the sweet, fresh rain in my face.
Diamonds and lace,
No got-so what?
For Robert Taylor I whistle and stamp.
That's why the lady is a tramp!

LITTLE GIRL BLUE

Sit there and count your fingers,
What can you do?
Old girl you're through.
Sit there and count your little fingers,
Unlucky little girl blue.

Sit there and count the raindrops
Falling on you.
It's time you knew,
All you can count on is the raindrops
That fall on little girl blue.
No use, old girl,
You may as well surrender.
Your hope is getting slender,
Why won't somebody send a tender
Blue boy to cheer a little girl blue?

When I was very young
The world was younger than I.
As merry as a carousel
The circus tent was strung
With every star in the sky
Above the ring I love as well.

Now the young world has grown old,
Gone are the tinsel and gold.

MY ROMANCE

I won't kiss your hand, madam,
Crazy for you though I am.
I'll never woo you on bended knee,
No, madam, not me.
We don't need that flowery fuss.
No sir, madam, not for us.

My romance doesn't have to have
A moon in the sky.
My romance doesn't need
A blue lagoon standing by.
No month of May, no twinkling stars.
No hideaway, no soft guitars.

My romance
Doesn't need a castle rising in Spain,
Nor a dance
To a constantly surprising refrain.
Wide awake,
I can make my most fantastic dreams
Come true.
My romance
Doesn't need a thing but you.

YOU ARE TOO BEAUTIFUL

You are too beautiful,
My dear, to be true,
And I am a fool for beauty;
Fooled by a feeling that
Because I had found you,
I could have bound you, too.

You are too beautiful
For one man alone,
For one lucky fool to be with,
When there are other men with
Eyes of their own to see with.

Love does not stand sharing,
Not if one cares.
Have you been comparing
My ev'ry kiss with theirs?
If on the other hand
I'm faithful to you,
It's not through a sense of duty;
You are too beautiful
And I am a fool for beauty.

THERE'S A SMALL HOTEL

Frankie:
I'd like to get away, Junior,
Somewhere alone with you.
It could be oh, so gay, Junior!
You need a laugh or two.

Junior:
A certain place I know, Frankie,
Where funny people can have fun.
That's where we two will go, darling,
Before you can count up
One, two, three
For...

There's a small hotel
With a wishing well;
I wish that we were there
Together.
There's a bridal suite;
One room bright and neat,
Complete for us to share
Together.

Looking through the window
You can see a distant steeple;
Not a sign of people,
Who wants people?
When the steeple bell says,
"Goodnight, sleep well,"
We'll thank the small hotel
Together.

Looking through the window
You can see a distant steeple;
Not a sign of people,
Who wants people?
When the steeple bell says,
"Goodnight, sleep well,"
We'll thank the small hotel.
We'll creep into our little shell
And we will thank the small hotel
Together.